EVERYDAY LIFE IN

ANCIENT EGYPT

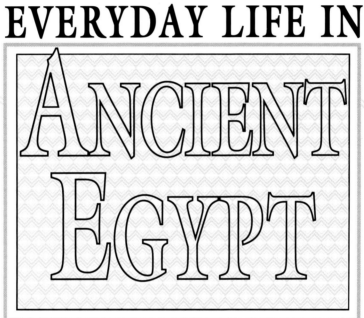

NATHANIEL HARRIS

FRANKLIN WATTS

LONDON•SYDNEY

This edition published in 2003 by
Franklin Watts
96 Leonard Street
London EC2A 4XD

Franklin Watts Australia
45-51 Huntley Street
Alexandria
NSW 2015

© 1993 Franklin Watts

ISBN 0 7496 2035 8

A CIP catalogue record for this book is available
from the British Library.

Editor: Sarah Ridley
Designer: Alan Cassedy
Illustrator: Kevin Maddison
Consultant: Delia Pemberton
Picture researcher: Joanne King

Photographs: British Museum front cover bl,
front cover cl, 6t, 10t, 12t, 23-13b, 14t, 16t, 18t, 20t, 22t, 26t;
Werner Forman Archive 4t, 7b, 8t, 24t, 28t; M Holford 6b, 30t;
Hulton-Deutsch Collection 7t

Printed in Dubai, UAE

CONTENTS

WHO WERE THE ANCIENT EGYPTIANS?

Egyptian civilisation began over 5,000 years ago, about the time when the first king united the two halves of the country. The Egyptians developed a way of life which lasted for over 3,000 years, impressing even the ancient Greeks and Romans with its great age and stability. Egypt was a land of many gods, and its kings, who became known as pharaohs, were regarded as living gods. Their absolute power enabled them to command the building of huge pyramids and temples for which Egypt is still famous.

Egyptian society was fixed and unchanging, with sons usually following their fathers' occupations. Apart from the pharaohs, the most important people were nobles, priests, and the scribes and officials who kept records and collected taxes. Then came craftsmen and other specialists. The great majority of Egyptians were simple peasant farmers.

Egyptian parents with their children, shown on a wall painting. As was customary, the children are naked and their heads are partly shaven. The long lock of hair over the right ear was a badge of childhood, worn until about the age of ten.

SOME IMPORTANT DATES IN ANCIENT EGYPTIAN HISTORY

Most of these events are so far back in time that the dates are only approximate.

EARLY PERIOD

5000 BC The earliest settlers appear on the Nile.

3100 BC Menes, King of Upper Egypt, conquers Lower Egypt. Hieroglyphic writing already developing.

OLD KINGDOM

2650 BC The first pyramid is built.
2575 BC The Great Pyramid is built for King Khufu, or Cheops.

MIDDLE KINGDOM

2060 BC Thebes becomes the capital of Egypt.
1780 BC Egypt invaded by a people from Asia, the Hyksos.

MEDITERRANEAN SEA

NILE DELTA

ANCIENT EGYPT

AFRICAN CONTINENT

Giza

Memphis•

RED SEA

RIVER NILE

Dendera

Abydos •

Thebes • • Karnak

NUBIAN DESERT

'THE GIFT OF THE NILE'

An ancient Greek historian called Egypt 'the gift of the Nile', because the river was the basis of its whole way of life. Running through a vast, almost rainless desert, the Nile fertilised the land beside its banks, and along this thin strip the Egyptians settled, became farmers, and created their great civilisation. Deserts, mountains and swamps limited Egypt's contact with the outside world, although she did eventually trade and wage wars beyond her frontiers. This was one important reason why the Egyptian way of life changed so little over thousands of years.

NEW KINGDOM

1567 BC Hyksos driven out.
1458 BC Tuthmosis III conquers Syria and Palestine.

1350 BC The pharaoh Akhenaten attempts to set up a new supreme god, the Aten.
1323 BC Death of the boy pharaoh Tutankhamen, famous because of the discovery of his tomb in 1922.

LATE PERIOD

525 BC Egypt is conquered by the Persians.
332 BC Conquest by Alexander the Great of Macedon (Greece).

323-30 BC The Ptolemies, a Greek dynasty, rule as pharaohs.
30 BC Egypt becomes part of Roman Empire.

We know a lot about the ancient Egyptians because large numbers of their records, pictures and personal possessions have survived. One reason for this is the climate, which is so dry that normally perishable things – documents, wooden objects, even bodies – have been preserved in the sand. Equally important was the Egyptians' belief in a life after death, which led them to put all sorts of everyday things into tombs for the dead person to use – things that tell us about many aspects of Egyptian life.

Rosetta Stone

IMMENSE STRUCTURES

Egypt is full of great structures such as pyramids, many-columned temples and obelisks (tall stone monuments). The pyramids were gigantic tombs, built for Egypt's kings. But they were robbed of their treasures so often that the pharaohs stopped building them and had themselves buried in hidden tombs cut from the cliffs of the Valley of the Kings, in the desert outside Thebes.

The pyramid at Chephren.

WRITTEN EVIDENCE

The Egyptians left behind them writings of many kinds – stories and poems as well as detailed factual records, descriptions of battles and books of religious instruction. However, the ancient Egyptian language died out, and no one could read it until the discovery of the Rosetta Stone (above). It carried three versions of the same text, inscribed in Greek and in two forms of Egyptian writing. Using the Greek – a known language – as his key, the French scholar Jean François Champollion was able to understand the Egyptian text, and in time the entire language was deciphered.

ARCHAEOLOGISTS AT WORK

The archaeologist digs up the buried past. He or she is often as interested in rubbish tips as in valuables, but sometimes really thrilling finds are made. The most sensational of all happened in 1922, when the British archaeologist, Howard Carter, discovered the tomb of the boy pharaoh, Tutankhamen. Every other royal tomb had been robbed long before, but Tutankhamen's was still full of priceless, superbly crafted gold and jewelled objects, revealing the incredible splendour of one of Egypt's 'living gods'.

PAINTING AND SCULPTURE

Painters worked within strict rules which seem rather strange to us (for example, always showing faces in profile, but with eyes seen from the front). But their pictures in books and paintings on walls are vivid and natural, portraying all sorts of scenes and activities. Large public sculptures are more formal, but family tomb monuments often show affectionate couples and groups.

Many humble little models have also survived which give us precious information about how things were made and used. Placed in tombs to represent the dead person's wealth and pleasures, they show people ploughing, sailing boats, in their homes and so on – life at its most everyday level.

ON THE NILE

This wooden model of a sailing boat shows the crew hard at work. The pilot stands in the bow (front), holding a weighted line which he can lower into the water to check its depth. In the stern, the steersman uses a long oar as a rudder. Meanwhile the owner sits at his ease under a canopy. Much of our knowledge of ancient Egypt comes from models like this one, found in tombs.

MAKING THE LAND FERTILE

The Nile served Egypt as a highway, a hunter's paradise and a pleasure resort. But above all the river gave the land its wonderful fertility. Every year, in mid-June, the Nile began to rise until it flooded its banks and covered the farmers' fields. After four months the water level fell again, leaving layers of rich earth which the river had brought down from the north. The crops grown in this soil provided the true wealth of Egypt. The Nile's behaviour was so vitally important that the Egyptians developed very accurate ways of recording and predicting it.

The Nile is about 5,600 kilometres long, rising far to the south of Egypt. In ancient times, rapids made sailing difficult until the First Cataract (waterfall) below Aswan had been passed. But then the river flowed gently north through the heart of Egypt, eventually splitting up in the flat Delta area and entering the sea.

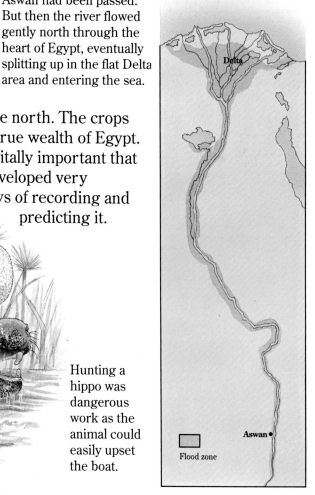

Hunting a hippo was dangerous work as the animal could easily upset the boat.

Delta

Flood zone

Aswan

LIFE ON THE NILE

Almost all Egyptians lived close to the Nile, which teemed with life. Hunters pursued the great variety of wild fowl with throwing sticks and nets. Fishermen hooked or netted their catches from light boats, made from tightly tied bundles of the papyrus reeds which grew along the riverbanks. Fiercer prey, such as hippopotamuses, were also to be found, especially in the marshy, untamed Nile Delta. Wealthy folk cruised the river for pleasure, and the Egyptians' vivid paintings of birds and beasts suggest that their beauty was keenly appreciated. The Nile was also a great waterway for vessels making longer journeys, carrying busy officials or transporting blocks of building stone.

In this busy river scene, large and medium-sized vessels transport goods, while fishermen in reed boats net a catch. On the bank, men hunt wildfowl with throwing sticks.

This fragment of a tomb painting shows herders bringing in their cattle to be inspected and counted. Cattle were among the most important sources of wealth – and of taxes for the government! On the left, scribes are recording the count: if any beast had died, the herder had to produce its hide in order to prove it had not been lost or stolen.

FRIENDS AND NEIGHBOURS

Egyptians lived very close to creatures of all kinds. A poor family might share their only room with the livestock, and even in bigger houses the living rooms, stalls and stables opened out into the same courtyard. People seem to have been fond of animals – paintings show them being stroked – and dogs, cats and monkeys were kept as pets. Two pharaohs, are said to have had their own private zoos.

Every kind of creature known to the Egyptians was also identified with one of their gods; for example, Hathor, the goddess of love and music, was usually shown as a cow. Animals even shared the human privilege – as the Egyptians viewed it – of being embalmed so that they survived into the afterlife. Archaeologists have discovered thousands of mummified animals.

OUT IN THE DESERT

Most Egyptians had little time for the dangerous 'red land' of the desert, preferring their own fertile 'black land' close to the Nile. But kings and nobles went out into the desert to hunt lions, wild bulls and elephants, to prove their courage rather than to find food. They also enjoyed chasing the flightless ostrich, a harmless bird with a surprising turn of speed. Better eating was provided by ostrich eggs, regarded as a great delicacy, and desert hares. Camels roamed wild and were not captured and domesticated until very late in Egyptian history, but unsuccessful attempts were made to tame ... the hyena!

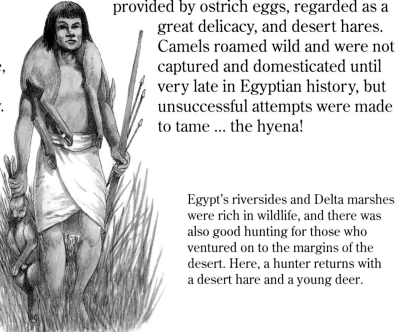

Egypt's riversides and Delta marshes were rich in wildlife, and there was also good hunting for those who ventured on to the margins of the desert. Here, a hunter returns with a desert hare and a young deer.

The cattleshed. In the left-hand stall, the beasts are being milked. To the right, a birth has just taken place.

BEASTS FOR USE AND FOR FOOD

The most valuable domesticated animals were cattle. There were large herds on the big estates, and fields of clover and other types of fodder were specially grown for them. Though put out to pasture during the day, they were shut up safely in sheds at nightfall. Poor people had few cattle, but raised goats, pigs and poultry.

A practical farming people, the Egyptians made most of their animals work for them, pulling ploughs or trampling seeds into the soil. Dogs were used for hunting, cats were trained to retrieve birds, and even monkeys became fruit-pickers! The horse was not introduced until late in Egyptian history, and even then remained a royal warrior's steed, leaving the donkey as the humble beast of burden.

Birds such as geese (below) and cranes were force-fed – that is, made to swallow unwanted food – to fatten them up for eating.

This tomb model shows an Egyptian farmer guiding his wooden plough. Ploughing was done to break up the rich, moist soil before it was sown with seeds. The blade of the light Egyptian plough did not cut very deep. This was fortunate since it meant that the precious moisture remained trapped in the upper layer of soil.

THE FARMER'S YEAR

The rise and fall of the Nile dominated farmers' lives. Every scrap of fertile land – land flooded by the Nile – was cultivated. Even the villagers' homes were built just outside the flood area, on the sand. During the four-month summer flood, farmers could relax, unless the state called them up to help build temples and pyramids. In autumn, after the flood had gone down, they ploughed and sowed the soil. Then in March came the harvest, perhaps followed by a second crop of vegetables before the next floods. The farmers' other main task was to maintain the dykes, canals and ditches which brought Nile water to the fields during the dry seasons.

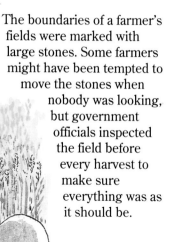

The boundaries of a farmer's fields were marked with large stones. Some farmers might have been tempted to move the stones when nobody was looking, but government officials inspected the field before every harvest to make sure everything was as it should be.

MAKING WINE
You must read each of these Egyptian pictures from right to left. The first strip shows grapes being picked from vines and carried away.

HARVESTING THE CROPS

In March, every able-bodied villager went out into the fields to harvest the crops. The men used their sickles to cut the stalks of corn. Women and children bundled them into sheaves and packed them into baskets, while others gleaned – went over the ground picking up anything the reapers had missed. Then the corn was threshed (broken down) and winnowed (thrown or sieved to separate the grain from the chaff) and stored.

The plough stands idle while the villagers harvest the rich crop. Even the children are recruited to help.

Here the grapes are being trampled with bare feet to release the juice, which is then stored in jars and left to ferment.

This lovely object is a girdle, designed to be worn loosely round a lady's waist. The metal parts are made of electrum, a gold-silver mixture. The beads are semi-precious stones of amethyst (violet), lapis lazuli (deep blue), turquoise (blue-green) and carnelian (orange-red). The girdle was rather like a large charm bracelet, with cowrie shells, and fish and hair-lock pendants, to guarantee good health and many children.

MADE TO LAST

Many of the things that survive from ancient Egypt are the work of craftsmen – potters, masons, carpenters, glassmakers, metalworkers and jewellers. Spinning and weaving, mainly done by women, were also skilled and important jobs, but the cloth they made has mostly perished. Painters and sculptors too were regarded as craftsmen, working along traditional lines, rather than 'artists'. Huge amounts of craftwork were done for the pharaohs, who kept an entire village of craftsmen in the Valley of the Kings, permanently employed in creating magnificent royal tombs.

Glass objects, like this fish, were made in a mould; the coloured stripes were added later. The pottery hippo is coated with a glassy substance called faience.

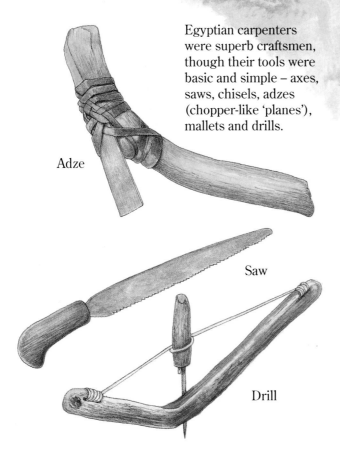

Metalworkers smelt, weigh, drill and hammer their materials.

Egyptian carpenters were superb craftsmen, though their tools were basic and simple – axes, saws, chisels, adzes (chopper-like 'planes'), mallets and drills.

Adze

Saw

Drill

METALWORKING

The Egyptians liked the golden glow of copper and bronze, and preferred them even after they knew about iron, which was much tougher. Solid gold objects were made only for the pharaohs and the great temples, but many other items were gilded – covered with a thin layer of gold.

The first step in working metals was smelting, which meant heating them over a fire to burn off impurities. Then the craftsmen beat the cold metal into the required shape or poured it, molten, into a mould. Scraping, rubbing down and polishing completed the job.

These are the tools of the trade used by scribes, who were Egypt's professional writers. The long wooden palette held black and red inks, and has a slot for the owner's reed pens; the other objects are a grinder for turning the colours into powder and a water pot for mixing them. As the brush-like pen and the colours suggest, Egyptian writing was rather like painting, and scribes tried to produce artistically satisfying work.

MANY DUTIES

Ancient Egypt was a highly organised society, dependent on detailed written records. Since most people could not read or write, the relatively small number of scribes had excellent career prospects! A local scribe might be paid to write letters or draw up contracts for his fellow-villagers, but others had more demanding jobs. They recorded the harvest and collected the state's share of it in taxes. They worked out the amounts needed to feed labourers on public works such as the pyramids. They kept the accounts on big estates and ordered supplies for the temples and the Egyptian army. Not surprisingly, scribes became Egypt's top managers and civil servants, qualified to hold any position.

SOME HIEROGLYPHICS

god   woman   man

small   strong

walk   limb   leather

wood   sun   pool

enemy   town   metal

TYPES OF WRITING

For really important purposes the Egyptians always used a very complicated script (writing system) known as hieroglyphics. There were over 700 hieroglyphic symbols, each like a little drawing; some were actually pictures of the things they stood for, while others represented sounds or groups of letters. Scribes had to master hieroglyphics, but to do their everyday work they developed a simplified script called hieratic, which could be written flowingly and quickly, like modern handwriting. Later still, hieratic was replaced by demotic, another simplified system; it is found, with hieroglyphics and Greek, on the Rosetta Stone (see page 6).

Scribes kept careful records of everything produced, acting as accountants and tax inspectors.

SCARAB SEALS

A seal was used to stamp a design in a material like clay.

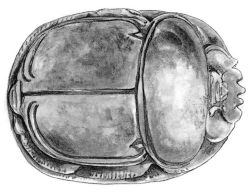

Some seals were made to commemorate a great event, such as the birth of a royal prince.

This one tells of a great lion hunt.

SCRIBES AT WORK

A scribe was often the son of a scribe, learning his skills from his father. But as more and more of them were needed, schools were set up for trainees. As well as hieroglyphics and hieratic writing, they learned subjects such as arithmetic, useful in an occupation which involved so much counting and calculating.

Schoolboys wrote their exercises on broken bits of pottery or wipe-off boards which could be used again. This was cheaper than papyrus, the material which scribes used for proper records and reports. Our word 'paper' comes from papyrus, a riverbank reed whose pith (inside) could be pounded into smooth sheets. Egyptian books were made in the form of scrolls, long sheets rolled up like wallpaper, which the scribe unwound with his left hand as he wrote.

Though crude-looking, this battle-axe is a formidable weapon, with a sturdy handle and a fine bronze blade inscribed in hieroglyphics. Egypt had special 'factories' for making weapons and, surprisingly, some of the most important of them were temples. When the Egyptians were about to go to war, a great ceremony was held in which weapons were piled up in front of the pharaoh and issued to the troops.

LATECOMERS TO WAR

For over a thousand years, the Egyptians had very little contact with other peoples. In times of emergency, armies were recruited from local peasants, who went home to their fields at the end of the campaign.

Eventually the Egyptians became more aggressive, and conquered parts of Nubia, to the south. But the real turning point came when Egypt was invaded by a people from Asia, the Hyksos, who ruled the Nile Delta for 200 years. The effort needed to drive them out seems to have encouraged new ideas of military glory. A regular army was established, and Egypt won an empire in Syria and Palestine. But after several hundred years of involvement in the Middle East, Egypt became a prize for more war-like states, and finally lost her independence altogether.

Egyptian infantrymen fought their enemies hand-to-hand with spears, knives and clubs, while warding off blows with their shields. Javelins and bows and arrows were the most important long-distance weapons.

Spear

Shield

Sword

Dagger

Bow and arrows

The army advances. The chariots will run down the enemy's infantry or encircle his army and attack from behind.

After a victory, the Egyptians counted the enemy dead – by piling up their severed hands. Prisoners, if they were lucky, were recruited into the Egyptian army. If they were unlucky, they too lost their hands (to stop them from ever fighting again) or were sold into slavery.

MOBILE WARFARE

The Egyptians learned from their enemies, the Hyksos, to use horses and chariots in battle. Warfare became more mobile, and conqueror-pharaohs such as Ramesses II relied heavily on their crack cavalry units. Pharaohs are usually pictured as alone and triumphant in their chariots, but in reality the driver was normally accompanied by an archer. The Egyptians also built warships to patrol the Nile. In the 12th century BC they played a decisive role in driving off the migrating 'Peoples of the Sea' who threatened to overrun Egypt.

This tomb model of a house is made of mud brick, just as real Egyptian houses were; stone was used only for temples and tombs. This is not a rich man's dwelling, but a respectable two-storey building with a wall round it. Models such as this one were placed in the tomb to be the dead person's home in the life after death, which is why they were called 'soul houses'.

HOME COMFORTS

Very poor people lived in reed huts, but most villagers had one or two-storey houses with several rooms. Once built with mud bricks, a house was finished off with a coat of plaster and painted decorations on the inside walls. Because of the hot climate, windows were small, keeping the house cool but dark. Families spent much of their leisure time on the roof, where vents in the balcony directed the breeze on to them. Wealthy people owned town houses and also country villas with tree-lined gardens and fish-stocked pools.

Most people had no furniture except a chest and some mats or mattresses. The rich owned elegant chairs, small tables, stools and beds. Using a bed was considered the sign of a superior person.

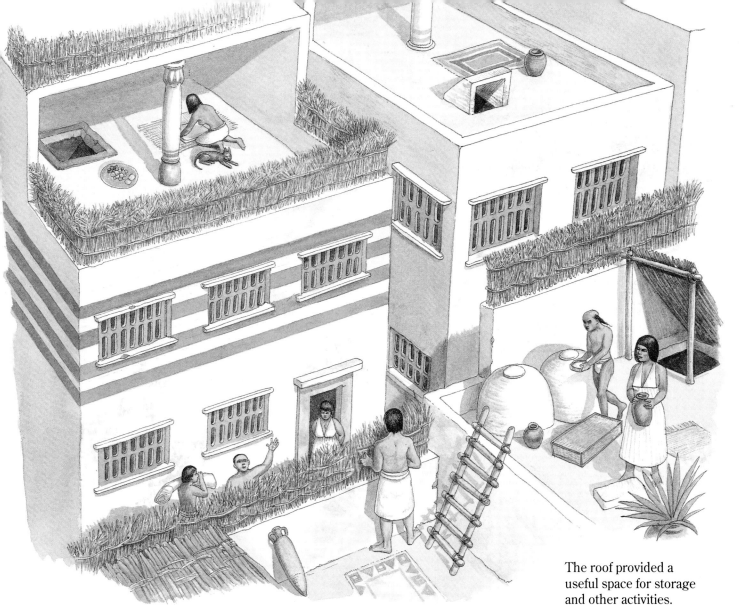

The roof provided a useful space for storage and other activities.

MAKING BRICKS

The basic material, mud, was carried in buckets from the nearest pool to the building site, and mixed with straw (or sometimes sand) to strengthen it. Then it was packed into hollow, brick-shaped wooden moulds. The bricks were left to set and harden in the fierce heat of the Egyptian sun.

TOWNS

Most Egyptian towns grew up, unplanned, around temples or palaces. In such towns the poorer quarters were very cramped and crowded, with small houses and a maze of winding streets. The rich lived in more spacious suburbs, but even here land was expensive, encouraging building upwards rather than along the ground. Houses might reach three storeys, with the main reception rooms on the first floor, above storerooms and craft workshops. The second floor held the owner's private apartments, while the roof provided additional storage space and, as always, a cool spot in which to sit or sleep out under an awning.

FOOD AND DRINK

This lavish spread of fruits, fowls and meat is part of a banquet scene, painted on a tomb wall. An equally vital feature of the entertainment was wine, stacked in rows of tall jars beside the food. Among the objects placed in Egyptian tombs were offerings of real food and drink. Thanks to the Egyptian climate, pieces of dried-up bread and fruit have been discovered in these tombs – still recognisable, if not very appetising!

ENOUGH FOR ALL

The fertility of the Nile valley ensured that everyone normally had enough to eat. The Egyptians' basic food and drink, bread and beer, were made from the main crops they grew, wheat and barley. Records mention 17 kinds of beer and over 50 types of bread, as well as pastries and cakes. Since there was no sugar, honey was used as a sweetener by the rich, and dates and fruit juices by the poor.

Egyptians liked strong-tasting vegetables such as garlic and onions, believing they were good for the health; but they also ate peas and beans, lettuce, cucumbers and leeks. Figs, dates and grapes were favourite fruits, but only the well-off could afford to make wine from their grapes. Ordinary people ate plenty of fish, some poultry and wild fowl when they could catch them; on special occasions they killed and cooked a sheep, goat or pig. The rich preferred beef, game birds, and exotic meats such as antelope.

Putting food aside for the future was a wise precaution, as long as it didn't go off. Grain could be stored, but fish, like meat, had to be specially prepared. One method was salting; another, even simpler, was to hang up the fish in the hot Egyptian sun, which baked them dry. Then the fish were packed away in ash to preserve them.

The hard work behind
the scenes. Making bread
and preparing choice fruits
for the feast.

PREPARING MEALS

In ordinary families the cooking was done by the housewife. But
larger households employed servants to work in the kitchen and a
chef – usually a man – to do the cooking. Making bread, brewing
and wine-making were all done on the spot. The Egyptians had
ovens, and also knew how to boil, roast and fry food. There were
few kitchen tools apart from pestles and mortars and sieves.

MAKING BREAD
The first step in bread-making
was to grind the corn into flour.

This was mixed
with water, yeast
and salt to make
dough, which was
kneaded with the
hands and left for
a time to rise.

Then the dough was
baked in a small oven.

At this banquet, shown on a tomb painting, two high-born ladies sit side by side in all their finery; one politely offers the other a lotus flower to smell. They are almost identically dressed and groomed – perhaps following the same fashion – with stylish wigs, huge earrings, heavily made-up eyes, wide collars and pleated gowns. Each carries a cone of scented fat on her head that will slowly melt in the heat, saturating her wig and head with a fragrant, refreshing moisture.

DRESS SENSE

For most of the time, Egypt was so hot that it was natural for people to wear as little as possible; children rarely wore clothes, and peasants, like servants and dancing girls, often worked nearly naked. Most men were content with a simple white linen or woollen kilt, while women wore long, close-fitting shifts made of similar materials. Nobles and their wives smartened up this basic outfit by having it neatly pleated and adding very light (sometimes see-through) cloaks and robes. Shapes and lengths varied with fashion, just as they do today.

To make up for the simplicity of their clothes, Egyptians wore a variety of wigs and all sorts of ornaments – head-bands, multi-rowed necklaces and collars, girdles, bangles, bracelets and rings. The rich glittered with precious stones and metals, while ordinary people made do with brightly coloured beads made of pottery or glass.

HAIR AND WIGS
Men and women wore their hair short, and men were almost always clean-shaven; even ordinary people went to the barber's. Priests shaved their heads completely. Wigs were worn by both sexes as fashionable extras and also as part of the required formal costume ('evening dress') on important occasions. There were professional wig-makers with their own workshops.

A grand lady makes herself up at the beginning of the day.

Applicators

Egyptian ladies had a variety of beauty aids which they carried about with them in cosmetic boxes.

Face cream pot

Bronze mirror

Perfume pot

THE QUEST FOR BEAUTY

Ladies of the upper class did everything they could to make themselves look fresh and attractive. They bathed often and had their bodies massaged with skin-softeners and sweetened with perfume. They used a dye called henna to redden their nails and hair. They made themselves up with kohl, a black substance with which they painted their eyebrows, outlined their eyes, and darkened their lashes. And, if they worried about ageing, they could try out the recipes that claimed to banish wrinkles!

An Egyptian child played with this little wooden cat over 3,000 years ago. It has a movable lower jaw and is one of several surviving figures with moving parts, including waggable tails. Among other toys were balls, tops, rattles, dolls and even miniature pieces of furniture – though no dolls' houses have been found so far! Poor children often made their own toys by whittling them out of wood or modelling them in mud and baking them in the sun.

SPORTS AND GAMES

Most popular sports and games were simple and cheap. Boys went in for all sorts of running, jumping and fighting, but seem to have left ball games to the girls. With water never far away, everybody enjoyed swimming. The upper classes hunted for pleasure and raced in their chariots; ordinary men competed against one another in athletics, wrestling and archery contests.

Board games were very popular – especially senet, which was played by both pharaohs and peasants, on beautiful inlaid boards or on squares scratched into the ground beside a village house. The rules of the game are not known but it seems to have been a bit like Chinese Chequers, with each player trying to cross the board while blocking his opponent's advance.

A number of toys used by Egyptian children have survived. Among them were balls made of clay, spinning tops, and pull-along models like the horse shown (below). They suggest that these children were not so very different from children today.

The gardens of the rich provided tranquil surroundings for a chat while the children played with their toys.

ENTERTAINMENT

Villagers often gathered to sing and make music, but when there was dancing, men and women never performed together. The Egyptians had no way of writing down their music, so we can only guess what it was like.

At expensive parties, the guests were entertained by professional musicians, scantily dressed dancing girls and acrobats. The host and hostess sat together, but male and female guests, were seated in separate groups, as were children. Like other party-goers, Egyptians tended to overeat, and some drank so much that they had to be carried home.

Egyptians often made music with everyday instruments such as flutes and pipes. Rattles, cymbals and drums beat out the rhythm for dancers. Wealthy people hired harpists, trumpeters and lyre-players. Instruments were never played by themselves, but always accompanied singers or dancers.

Cymbals

Flute

Lyre

Many Egyptian gods were portrayed as animals, or as human beings with animal heads. This granite statue stands outside the Temple of Horus, Edfu, guarding the entrance to the inner sanctum. It is the sky-god Horus the Elder, who is shown as a falcon; his eyes are the sun and moon. The pharaoh was identified with Horus, whom he represented on earth. Egyptian religion was very complicated, and Horus was also a child-god, son of Osiris and Isis. Among other gods and goddesses which took animal form were Bastet, the cat goddess and the ibis-headed Thoth, god of wisdom.

Worn to fend off evil, an amulet invoked the protection of a god for its wearer. Among the most powerful symbols were the beautifully designed single eye of Horus and the scarab beetle, often shown with wings, which represented the sun.

LAND OF MANY GODS

There were hundreds of gods and goddesses in Egypt, watching over every aspect of life and death. This seemed natural to the Egyptians, who were outraged when the pharaoh Akhenaten tried to make them worship a single god. After his death, Akhenaten was cursed by the priests and the old ways were taken up.

The greatest of all the gods was Re, the life-giving sun god and father of the pharaoh, who was himself regarded as a living god. Egyptians were also vitally concerned with Osiris, a god who had died and been brought back to life by his wife Isis; now the lord of the underworld, he would be their judge after death.

A religious procession moves through the inner courtyard of a temple to the god Horus. The small cult figure of Horus is protected inside the golden shrine.

The sistrum was a metal rattle used by priestesses during religious ceremonies. An image of Hathor, goddess of music, often appeared on its handle.

TEMPLES

Egypt was a land of mighty temples, built at the command of the pharaohs. Owning huge estates and equipped with schools, workshops, granaries and libraries, temples were thriving, busy places. But only priests and priestesses were allowed into the heart of the temple – the dim sanctuary where the god dwelt. Every day the god's image was dressed, washed and 'fed' with offerings, but the people saw it only at great festivals, when it was paraded up and down for miles around.

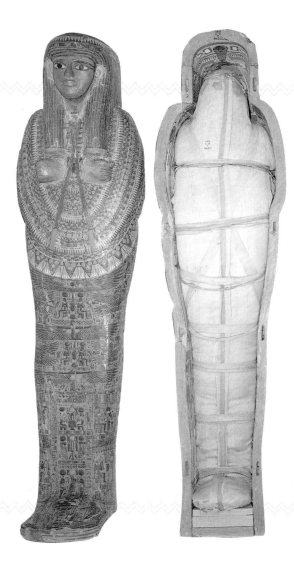

This coffin has been carved and painted to resemble the dead person, a priestess from Thebes. An important figure such as a pharaoh was buried in a set of superbly decorated coffins, one inside another.

The Egyptians believed that death was the threshold to eternal life, which was ensured by performing elaborate magical ceremonies. And since the tomb would be the dead person's home for eternity, it was furnished as luxuriously as possible. It was also vital that the body should survive, and so it was mummified – given a special treatment, called embalming, to stop it from decaying.

MAKING A MUMMY

Mummification was skilled work, but it was also a religious ritual, carried out by priestly embalmers and accompanied by chants and spells. In the embalming workshop, the liver and other internal organs were removed, dried out, and sealed up in special jars. Then the body was packed in crystals of a chemical called natron, which dried and preserved it. Now a mummy, it was wrapped in linen bandages and covered with the mask, ready for the dead person's soul to re-enter it.

Among the most useful objects placed in an Egyptian's tomb were little figures called *shabtis* or *shawabtis*. If the dead person was ordered to do any work in the afterlife, he – or she – could get the *shabtis* to do it instead!

As the mourners wail, a priest prepares to 'open the mouth' of the dead person.

BACK TO LIFE

Just before the dead person was laid in the tomb, the priests performed the 'opening of the mouth' ceremony. They stood the coffin upright and touched its face with various instruments. This brought the mummy back to life, enabling it to breathe, see and enjoy itself in its new 'eternal house', the tomb.

These human and animal-headed jars, called canopic jars, held the dead person's internal organs and were placed in the tomb along with the body. Each head represented a son of the god Horus and protected a specific organ.